Evergreen Dreams

Adil Cassam Oozeerally

BookLeaf Publishing

Presentation by *BookLeaf Publishing*

Web: www.bookleafpub.com

E-mail: info@bookleafpub.com

ISBN: 9789357696845

First edition 2023

DEDICATION

I would like to dedicate this book to six year old Adil, I love you.

ACKNOWLEDGEMENT

I'd like to acknowledge Nature first and foremost, for being the greatest inspiration that will ever exist. I'd like to say a special thank you to Walid, Conor, Alvin, Sherif, Dhruv, Hannah and Milly for all their help and support while I worked on this book. Thank you to everybody who owns a copy of this book - you ought to know that writing poetry was never about publishing it, it was about immortalising feelings and moments into words. Creating for the joy of creating, nothing more, nothing less.

PREFACE

Evergreens are one of the two Taoist Trees of Life - representing resilience and adaptability. Spiritually speaking they are symbolic of eternal life. To the people of Iroquois they are a symbol of peace.

Evergreen Dreams is an ode to perennial dreams, undying and beautiful. To staying positive in the face of negativity. To staying true to yourself. To keeping it together when all else around you falls to the ground. To everlasting love and happiness.

The majority of the poems in this book were written in a twenty one day span in the Autumn of 2022. They reflect my thoughts and feelings at the time. They reflect the events and experiences I faced during this three week period. They reflect the people in my life and their impact on my life. They are pieces of my mind, that through writing, have contributed to peace of my mind.

Echoes and Answers

Who is asking?
  it is I.

Why do you seek?
  to find You.
Where will you go?
  inwards.
What will you see?
  nothing.
What will you hear?
  Everything.
What do you want?
  to know why.
What do you need?
  to not know.

Why did you ask?
  to see if You would reply.

Yin Yang

Since I was seven
I debated heaven,
from eleven
I lost God's lesson
I had a inner question
a quiet confession:

That if I was good,
would I make paradise
with my religion paralysed?
That god as an answer
didn’t quite suffice.

I felt unwise as
the world comprised
Christ or a Reverend
is the price to heaven,
that if it wasn’t paid
then in hell I’d wait
locked from God’s gate
til fire set me straight,
but can you force faith
or fake fate to state case
that God’s grace will embrace
when you find your place

like water to a vase.

What if Jesus needs us?
What if he's within us?
are we all Gods
kept from connecting dots?

it's easier to lead
those that follow
than those that show
signs of unity,
I almost felt lunacy
being truthfully humanly
I hollowly prayed
blindly I strayed,
without faith I was caged
to a religion I betrayed,
trying my best to evade
those that didn't relate
to how I saw faith,
I couldn't state my view
didn't know what was true,
another turn of the screw.

Was it the Big Bang?
Or is it all God's plan?

But then I saw Yin Yang
and the balance it sang

the same balance we hang
so my first thoughts sprang:

That the clues in you.
That you choose the world you view.
That God's not in you but God is you.

I believe this is true,
I believe if you leave
the outsiders view
you'll soon see who
you were all along,
that we sing the same song
that there's no right or wrong
it all blends into one
and one becomes all
and all becomes one.

Be You, Be True

Do evergreens
 ever dream
 of turning brown?
Do futile fish
 ever wish
 of wanting to drown?
Do the lost
 ever hope
 to not be found?
Do the silent
 ever think
 of making a sound?

Sometimes the signs
don't always show,
anomalies probably
chose to be so,
you don't have to see
 what is always shown
you don't have to be
 what you've always known.

Blood of a Poet

I never knew you
your name was a whisper,
we didn't discuss family ties
and I never knew why,
it wasn't until this July
I took a look at this book
laid to rest on my desk
it was tattered and torn
it's pages yellow and worn,
full of poetry unknown to me
yet the words seem familiar
and the poems seemed similar
to ones I had written,
it was titled Borderland
written by the hand of a man
named Michael Cubitt
and that's when I knew it -
my eyes recognised that name
and so did the blood in my veins
for what runs in them
is what ran through you
you were the Grandfather I never knew.

So I sat and read cover to cover
trying to uncover every clue

learning what I could about you,
I thought it was just me
who wrote poetry in our family,
but there it sat on my lap
84 pages of poems and stories
of your sadness and glories,
and in 1956 you published it
and 66 years later it sits
in my hands and heart
I am so grateful for your art.

So here and now I make a vow
to publish my poems in a book that
one day my grandchild can look at,
he'll turn to his dad so glad
and say he had always known it
that he has the blood of a poet.

Under The Sun

I am searching for my calling
looking within and falling,
like a child I am crawling
learning to move before walking,
so I think before speaking
knowing what I sow
is what I'll be reaping,
I start dreaming
outside of sleeping,
believing what we think
we become,
that life isn't a race
so don't run,
live at your own pace
and have fun,
live with grace
and know we are one
all has its place
under the Sun.

Vehemence Presence

Some nights I can't write.

I drown in feelings
that I dare not fight
or press against ceilings
and push with all my might,
but I realised
we must feel rather than hide
we must dive deep inside
where the emotions reside,
and conjure the courage
to free fall through them all,
to honestly hold each one
and unfold it's layers
until it comes undone,
and when it's laid bare
learn why it's there
treat it just and fair
cradle it with care,
let the feelings flow
then let them go
and know it's true
that you have feelings
they don't have you.

River Song

You took me to the river
so we may listen together
to the sounds of the water
carrying the sounds of all,
you asked if I could hear it,
I leaned in so closely
you were scared I'd fall
and I asked
would it be so bad if I had?

Why are we so scared to fall
when it is only natural after all,
falling in love and falling asleep,
falling feet first into the deep.

So I sat back and watched that
river run wildly free
listening to the sounds that be,
dipping my hand in
letting the water surround it
and realising I'll never touch
this same current again,
similar to my soul
dipping itself in my body
letting this world surround it

to realise it'll never be
in this same time and place again.

Swollen Emotions

a sadness swells inside me
 while happiness sits besides me,
it swells and swarms
and warns of storms
 while happiness sits besides me,
it's dark and deep
and rarely sleeps
 while happiness sits besides me,
it's grainy and grey
and has much to say
 while happiness sits besides me,
but if I write down
the way sadness sounds
 then happiness sits inside me,
and if I say aloud
what forms this cloud
 then happiness sits inside me,
and if I know
that to feel sorrow
meant I was happy then
and I will be happy again
 then happiness sits inside me,
and now I know
that joy will grow
as deeply as sadness cut me,

so I welcome the sorrow
today and tomorrow
and happiness swells inside me.

Droplets

in the early morning
as the Sun began to rise
with sleep clouded eyes
I stood there pouring
water into a glass,
until a drop sat on the brim
and as quick as lightning
there landed a big grin,
I stared and realised
there is no difference
from this drop that was last
to all of it in the glass,
that we aren't different souls
in different people
we are one and the same
not greater just equal,
that each spirit
carries with it
the source of that
undying never lying force.

As that drop fell
I smiled and knew
what is in me
is in you too.

Bodybuilding

We were made for nature
not these four walls
no wonder we are unhappy
ee can't hear natures calls,
Our toes
should feel soft grass
instead we have cold concrete,
Our eyes
should see clear skies
instead we see it through glass,
Our skin
should feel the wild wind
instead we don't feel a thing,
Our ears
should hear beautiful birds
instead we hear cars,
Our nose
should smell fragrant flowers
instead we smell pollution.

We were not made
for what we have built,
we built for the mind
but not for the heart
we built for the body
but not for the soul.

Our Little Pond

Come with me
and step out of time
let us see
what we might find,
hidden deep in this rhyme
is the moral of the story
that is told before me.

Place your mind
In a fallible animal,
born in a pond
very fond of food
has a few rivals
survival its only mood.

Now does this creature
have the feature
to conceive the sea?
Or can it be that possibly
all it knew is where it grew?
Do you fit that shoe?
If so then,
you were meant to hear this
just know when
death is nearest

you'll see clearest
so drop the realist
and just feel this,
if you implore
you will see
you are so much more
powerful and pure
all the way to the core.

Before you're stuck in the pond
it's not where we belong,
trust in the motion
believe there's an ocean.

I Call Mine Brian

Close your eyes,
breathe and realise
that what you think lies
behind your two eyes
is not your entire self.

It is merely a looking glass
holding concepts of future
present and past,
it has thoughts and sorts
knowledge into sections
but it is purely a reflection
of the time it's spent
in this environment.

That like a projection
you control what you see
think and feel,
that the pain you grasp
just needs time to heal,
though time is the doctor
it is not the medicine
and therein lies the secret
that the elixir is within.

So don't be ridiculed
or fooled by this tool
but learn to use it
or slowly lose it,
for its imagination
is wider than the sky
and wisdom sits at its tip
if you start questioning why.

So I request once more
to explore that which lies
behind your two eyes
and recognise you are not it
though in your body it may sit
it doesn't own you
you own it.

Dancer and Rhythm

A bird bred in captivity
doesn't know that it's wings
are the things
that can set it free,
it sings of skies it will never see
of wind it's wings will never feel
of sights so vividly vast
few others can surpass.

Imagine if we could grasp
the concept to forget the past,
the future too and for a few
moments let the movements
of the Earth take place
feel the birth of nature's pace,
every slice of life is different
each with the answer hidden
like a dancer to the rhythm
you must feel not think
plant your heels and sink,
feel the beat of your heart
know soul and body are apart,
yet part of the one whole
where every soul is the same,
we may be the painting
but the Oneness is the frame.

Signposts

Things occur when they should
they birth themselves
when they are ready
they present themselves
when we are ready,
a moment sooner
 and we may miss it's value
a moment later
 and we may miss it entirely.

They occur
 as signs,
they occur
 as words,
they occur
 as people,
they occur
 as events,
they occur
 as thoughts,
they occur
 as feelings,
they occur.

We must ready ourselves

for when they occur
because the path is long
but the journey is easy,
for those who are ready
for those who understand
for those who see themselves
in everything else,
then everything is a sign
everything occurs
as it should
when it should
for the greater good.

Eye of the Beholder

You spot a flight
of three geese
and breathe the peace
of what's around
as it echoes and surrounds
all who listen to its sound.
Seeing this makes you wonder
perhaps what makes
a day beautiful
isn't divine sunshine
separating clouds
leaving sparkles
to dance upon water,
perhaps it's you
that makes the day beautiful,
what if the day
just needs you to say
out loud just how
beautiful it is now.

You looked down
at the water's surface
and saw yourself
in the rippled reflection
you uttered a question:

what if beholding beauty
is neither chance nor duty
but a simple transition
in your recognition
of what is beautiful?

Then when you recognise
that beauty lies in everything
you'll start to see it everywhere
and you'll find that every day
beauty is on display in every way.

Same Time Different Places

I used to get sad
thinking about the times
that we could have had
times where I needed you,
where the sky fell down on me
the stars stopped blinking
the birds stopped singing
and I was sinking in overthinking.

But there's something freeing
when analysis paralysis
holds your entire being,
because thinking led to silence
and from quiet comes the truth
of finding what we lost after youth,
before ego had control
you'd go where happiness flows
to the places where time slows
and your beautiful aura glows
with the glee that comes
from being free.

But you grew up and threw out
that lack of self doubt,
instead of wanting to be better

than yourself
you just want to be better
than everyone else,
you no longer look inner
your eyes lose their glimmer
your aura becomes dimmer
your smile grows thinner,
so instead of learning
to love yourself
you try and love someone else.

So unfolds cynical cycles
of fragile trust, vicious lust
and intimacy with no purpose
other than to hurt us,
until you find yourself
standing in the rain
waiting for a train
heart full of blues and pain
praying not to go through it again.

You get up the next morning
cross legged and yawning
closing your eyes, drawing
a slow and gentle breath
flowing into your depths,
you awake from meditation
with the sensation
that today marks the steps

you will take to progress
to become your highest version,
you know now that
to meet the right person
you must become the right person.

So you spend time in nature
and reflect on becoming greater
what it means to live a life so serene
your dreams seem dim in comparison,
you work on becoming complete
without the need to compete
for another souls attention,
you find beauty all around you
within you and in others,
you find happiness in the small
and the ocean of self love
in which you sink and fall.

I used to get sad
now I am nothing
but happy and at peace
from things I used to wish,
and despite there being
moments and memories
where you don't exist,
the truth is that you do
I just haven't had the pleasure
of meeting you.

H is for

Poetry seems to be
written emotionally
and sadness is openly
placed upon pages of poets,
but to me there is one emotion
that unlike sadness
is not an ocean
of unknown depths
filled with dark waters
surrounding a fortress.

Instead it is
as wide as the sky
and gifts wings to fly,
like a gilded staircase
of infinite steps
with each step taken
this emotion awakens,
it stirs from its nest
and births a little light
that sits inside my chest
and each fibre
fills with wildfire
as it spreads to the rest,
and so it sheds

the weight of stress and
pain of depression
and a similar impression
is left on those exposed
to this healing feeling,
it is a path you can take
to elevate your mind state
but you must choose it
or you'll lose it
it has no price
and belongs to no place
but can be found on your face
in the form of a smile
full of endless bliss
it is called happiness.

03:08 2016

Have you ever sat down and
thought about what makes you smile
when no one is around
and makes you so happy
it lifts you off the ground?

To me we are humans
who lost humanity
while chasing greed
and things to feed our ego
but that's not real though,
nobody just wants to be.

You see we will
always want more
always think we are poor
if we compare to the man next door,
it's only in retrospect
that we regret we let
others tell us what we need,
let them lead our dreams
instead of being a team
instead of shining together
through the worst of weather,
whether we need support

from battles we fought
or to share a thought or two
about the wars you been through,
we have no clue from first glances
who's been given second chances
for their dances with the devil
and a medal of honour
for killing a foreigner
doesn't make you strong
if what you're doing is wrong,

While I write this one
I am reminded
that if you stand for nothing
you will fall for anything
or anyone with a forked tongue
who forces their view
that is very rarely true,
too few believe in themselves
and remain enslaved
in the hells they made
never to be saved
til the day before the grave
where they wish they paid
more attention to the moments
that took their breath away,
for your own sake
remember life isn't about
how many breaths you take

or those who forsake you
it's about happiness and love
and that's all it takes
to make your world great
so when your heart does break
and you get knocked down
remember you are a royalty
with or without a crown
and that frown
turn it upside down because
the only certainty in life is death
and when you feel unblessed
put a hand on your chest
and feel the beat of your heart
live your life like an art
and with every first impression
and every expression
and a stroke of paint to the page
no matter your age
don't be afraid
to be true
to you.

Come and Go

I had a Sunday stroll
just the other day
during a lonely lull
while life was tinted grey,
until a butterfly
fluttered on by
landed on my finger
lingered and left,
while I watched it go
I smiled and caught
the following thought
that if something comes
then I should let it,
be humble in its presence
and be present with it
for a second or century,
and if it should go
then I better let it
for it is not meant for me.

Little Lessons of Love

If time is a circle
and everything
that can happen
has happened
and everything that
has happened
is yet to happen -
then I am a caesura
between my future child
and the one in the past,
so I write this for you both
with the hope it helps
and I hereby make an oath
to love you with my entire self.

First and foremost,
leave wealth on the shelf
prioritise your inner self
and take care of your health,
if you chase monetary happiness
know it's path is endless
joy will merely be momentary
before you look for more,
so instead I ask that you implore
bring yourself peace like the dove

look within and find the finer things
that fill you to the brim with love,
follow these treasures of the soul
and measure them not with a goal
but just find pleasure in them all
and upwards you will fall.

I hope you inherit my kindness
and know that selfishness
has no place in love
it is through selflessness
you will feel God's hug,
I hope you climb trees
and scrape your knees
let your imagination sail
with love as it's breeze,
I recommend you find a friend
with whom you can face each test
one who knows you to the end
one you can call your best,
I hope you see beauty in the broken
that you are honest and open
and if not for anyone else
then at least be so with yourself.

I hope with your Mother it's okay
if I sing you songs each day,
and someday listen while you play
if music is the sound of the soul

then an instrument is a doorway,
I hope to read to you
the tales of Pan and Hook
and secretly feed to you
the wonders held in books,
that the one who reads
lives so many lives
until the day he dies
but those who read none
will only live one.

It is with great love and hope
that I leave you with a final note
that doing good ripples good,
learn to love yourself
before you love anyone else,
accept every part of you
and know you deserve happiness too,
and of all my wisdom shared
I hope you will recall
that it's better to live and love
then to never live at all.

Life's a Blink

I blinked and I was born,
crying and screaming
from the warmth I was torn
awoken from dreaming.

I blinked and I was ten,
playing with my best friend
blissfully carefree
our imagination had no end.

I blinked and I was sixteen,
dreams longer than my hair
chasing love but found lust
believing life isn't fair.

I blinked and I was twenty,
mind opened but not empty
still believing I knew it all
ready to jump but not to fall

I blinked and I was twenty seven,
the worst year of them all
yet the best year I recall,
lessons in abundance
friendships fewer but fiercer.

I lost my good health
I stopped chasing wealth,
I read more and wrote more,
I spent more time alone
I made my body a home,
my mind a temple
my soul more gentle.

I will blink and be at deaths door
and I hope I am smiling
before I am lowered into the floor,
I hope I don't ask for more
that I had my fill and I'm sure
I'll remember the golden days,
the childhood spent playing
the adolescence spent feeling
the adulthood spent growing
the marriage spent loving
the fatherhood spent caring.

Before I walk through that door
I will blink and blink no more.